Winter

Discover the Flavors of Winter with
Delicious Winter Recipes in a Delicious
Winter Cookbook

By
BookSumo Press

Published by
http://www.booksumo.com

LEGAL NOTES

Table of Contents

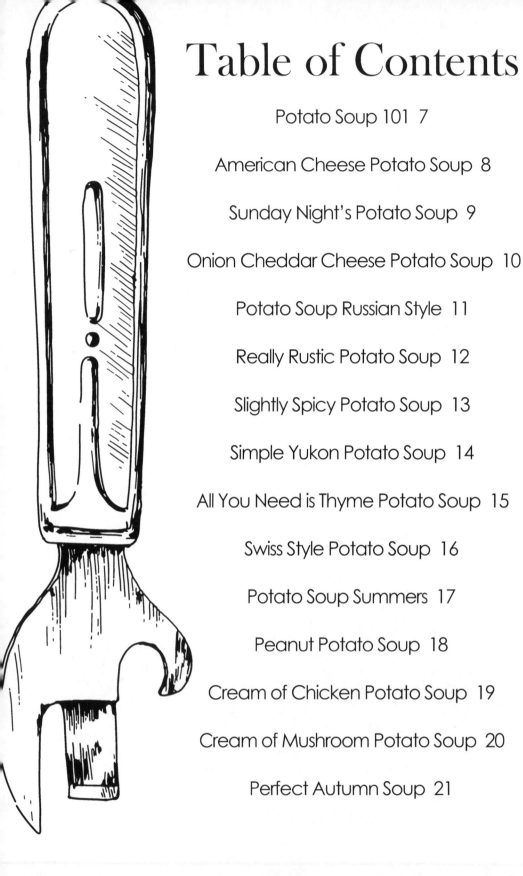

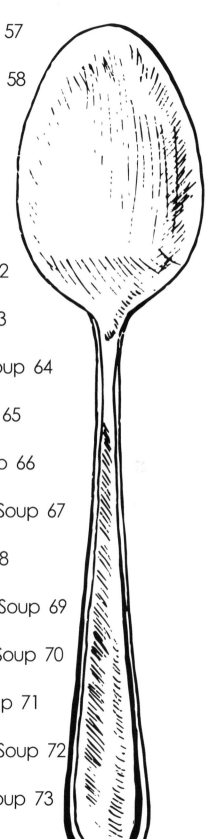

Potato Soup
101

Prep Time: 15 mins
Total Time: 1 hr

Servings per Recipe: 12

Calories	241 kcal
Fat	15.3 g
Carbohydrates	22.5g
Protein	4.5 g
Cholesterol	45 mg
Sodium	469 mg

Ingredients

6 C. diced potatoes
3 stalks celery, diced
1 C. chopped onion
3 (14.5 oz.) cans chicken broth, divided
4 C. half-and-half cream
6 tbsp butter, melted
6 tbsp all-purpose flour

4 cubes chicken bouillon
1/2 tsp ground black pepper

Directions

1. In a large pan, add the potatoes, celery, onion and 2 C. of the broth and bring to a boil.
2. Cook the potatoes for about 15 minutes.
3. Drain and reserve the liquid.
4. In a pan, mix together the reserved broth and half-and-half.
5. In a bowl, mix together the melted butter and flour.
6. Add the flour mixture into the butter mixture and stir to combine.
7. Add the flour mixture into the half-and-half mixture and mix well on medium heat.
8. Cook, stirring continuously till the mixture becomes thick.
9. Stir in the reserved vegetables, remaining broth, bouillon and pepper and cook till heated completely.

CLASSICAL
American Cheese Potato Soup

 Prep Time: 25 mins
Total Time: 1 hr 15 mins

Servings per Recipe: 8
Calories	299 kcal
Fat	14.7 g
Carbohydrates	24.3g
Protein	16.5 g
Cholesterol	57 mg
Sodium	1389 mg

Ingredients

3 C. peeled and cubed potatoes
1/2 C. chopped celery
1/2 C. chopped onion
1 cube chicken bouillon
1 C. water
1 tsp dried parsley

1/2 tsp salt
1 pinch ground black pepper
2 tsp all-purpose flour
1 1/2 C. milk
1 1/2 C. shredded American cheese
1 C. chopped turkey

Directions

1. In a large soup pan, add the potatoes, celery, onion, chicken bouillon, water, parsley flakes, salt and pepper and simmer till the vegetables become tender.
2. In a bowl mix together the flour and milk.
3. Add the flour mixture into the soup mixture and cook till the soup becomes thick.
4. Stir in the cheese, cooked turkey and simmer till the cheese is melted.

Sunday Night's Potato Soup

Prep Time: 20 mins
Total Time: 45 mins

Servings per Recipe: 8	
Calories	195 kcal
Fat	10.5 g
Carbohydrates	19.5g
Protein	6.1 g
Cholesterol	30 mg
Sodium	394 mg

Ingredients

3 1/2 C. peeled and diced potatoes
1/3 C. diced celery
1/3 C. finely chopped onion
3/4 C. diced cooked turkey, optional
3 1/4 C. water
2 tbsp chicken bouillon granules
1/2 tsp salt

1 tsp ground white pepper
5 tbsp butter
5 tbsp all-purpose flour
2 C. milk

Directions

1. In a soup pan, mix together the potatoes, celery, onion, turkey and water n medium heat and bring to a boil.
2. Cook for about 10-15 minutes.
3. Stir in the chicken bouillon, salt and pepper.
4. In another pan, melt the butter on medium-low heat.
5. Slowly, add the flour, beating continuously.
6. Cook, stirring continuously for about 1 minute.
7. Slowly add the milk, stirring continuously on medium-low heat.
8. Cook, stirring continuously for about 4-5 minutes.
9. Add the milk mixture into the soup pan and stir to combine.
10. Cook till heated completely.
11. Serve immediately.

GREEN ONION
Cheddar Cheese Potato Soup

Prep Time: 15 mins
Total Time: 40 mins

Servings per Recipe: 6

Calories	748 kcal
Fat	49.3 g
Carbohydrates	49.7g
Protein	27.2 g
Cholesterol	85 mg
Sodium	1335 mg

Ingredients

12 slices turkey bacon, optional
2/3 C. margarine
2/3 C. all-purpose flour
7 C. milk
4 large baked potatoes, peeled and cubed

4 green onions, chopped
1 1/4 C. shredded Cheddar cheese
1 C. sour cream
1 tsp salt
1 tsp ground black pepper

Directions

1. Heat a large skillet on medium heat and cook the bacon till browned completely.
2. Transfer the bacon onto a paper towel lined plate to drain and then crumble it.
3. In a soup pan, melt the margarine on medium heat.
4. Slowly, add the flour beating continuously till smooth.
5. Slowly, stir in the milk, beating continuously till thickened.
6. Stir in the potatoes and onions and bring to a boil, stirring occasionally.
7. Reduce the heat and simmer for about 10 minutes.
8. Stir in the bacon, cheese, sour cream salt, and pepper.
9. Cook, stirring occasionally till the cheese is melted.

Potato Soup
Russian Style

Prep Time: 20 mins
Total Time: 1 hr

Servings per Recipe: 12

Calories	167 kcal
Fat	7.7 g
Carbohydrates	21.2g
Protein	4.5 g
Cholesterol	23 mg
Sodium	928 mg

Ingredients

5 tbsp butter, divided
2 leeks, chopped
2 large carrots, sliced
6 C. chicken broth
2 tsp dried dill weed
2 tsp salt
1/8 tsp ground black pepper

1 bay leaf
2 lb. potatoes, peeled and diced
1 lb. fresh mushrooms, sliced
1 C. half-and-half
1/4 C. all-purpose flour
fresh dill weed, for garnish

Directions

1. In a large pan, melt the butter on medium heat and cook the leeks and carrots for about 5 minutes.
2. Add the potatoes, broth, dill, salt, pepper and bay leaf and cook, covered for about 20 minutes.
3. Remove from the heat and discard the bay leaf.
4. In a skillet, melt the remaining butter on medium heat and sauté the mushrooms for about 5 minutes.
5. Stir the mushrooms into the soup.
6. In a small bowl, mix the half-and-half and flour till smooth.
7. Stir into the soup to thicken.
8. Serve with a garnishing of fresh dill.

REALLY RUSTIC
Potato Soup

Prep Time: 20 mins
Total Time: 50 mins

Servings per Recipe: 8
Calories	594 kcal
Fat	41.5 g
Carbohydrates	44g
Protein	12.6 g
Cholesterol	91 mg
Sodium	879 mg

Ingredients

1 lb. turkey bacon, chopped, optional
2 stalks celery, diced
1 onion, chopped
3 cloves garlic, minced
8 potatoes, peeled and cubed
4 C. chicken stock

3 tbsp butter
1/4 C. all-purpose flour
1 C. heavy cream
1 tsp dried tarragon
3 tsp chopped fresh cilantro
salt and pepper to taste

Directions

1. Heat a large Dutch oven on medium heat and cook the bacon till browned completely.
2. Transfer the bacon onto a paper towel lined plate to drain.
3. Drain the bacon grease from the pan, leaving about 1/4 C inside.
4. Cook the celery and onion in reserved bacon drippings for about 5 minutes.
5. Stir in garlic, and cook for about 1-2 minutes.
6. Add the cubed potatoes and toss to coat and sauté for about 3-4 minutes.
7. Return the bacon to the pan and add chicken broth to just cover the potatoes.
8. Simmer, covered till the potatoes become tender.
9. In another pan, melt the butter on medium heat.
10. Slowly, add the flour, beating continuously.
11. Cook, stirring continuously for about 1-2 minutes.
12. Add the heavy cream, tarragon and cilantro and beat to combine.
13. Bring the cream mixture to a boil and cook, stirring continuously till the mixture becomes thick.
14. Stir the cream mixture into the potato mixture.
15. In a blender, add about 1/2 of the soup and pukes till pureed.
16. Return the pureed soup to the pan and adjust the seasonings to taste.

Slightly Spicy Potato Soup

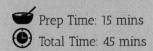

Prep Time: 15 mins
Total Time: 45 mins

Servings per Recipe: 6

Calories	366 kcal
Fat	29.6 g
Carbohydrates	16g
Protein	10.4 g
Cholesterol	99 mg
Sodium	348 mg

Ingredients

2 tbsp butter
1 C. diced onion
2 1/2 C. peeled and diced potatoes
3 C. chicken broth
1 C. heavy cream
1 3/4 C. shredded sharp Cheddar cheese
1/4 tsp dried dill weed

1/4 tsp ground black pepper
1/4 tsp salt
1/8 tsp ground cayenne pepper

Directions

1. In a large pan, melt the butter on medium heat and cook the onion till softened.

2. Stir in the potatoes and broth and bring to a boil.

3. Reduce the heat and simmer, covered for about 15-20 minutes.

4. With an immersion blender, puree the potato mixture.

5. Place the pan on medium heat and stir in the cream, cheese, dill, pepper, salt and cayenne.

6. Bring to a low boil and cook, stirring continuously for about 5 minutes.

SIMPLE
Yukon Potato Soup

 Prep Time: 15 mins
Total Time: 1 hr 15 mins

Servings per Recipe: 8

Calories	488 kcal
Fat	45.4 g
Carbohydrates	18.7g
Protein	3.7 g
Cholesterol	145 mg
Sodium	673 mg

Ingredients

1 C. butter
2 leeks, sliced
salt and pepper to taste
1 quart chicken broth
1 tbsp cornstarch
4 C. Yukon Gold potatoes, peeled and
diced
2 C. heavy cream

Directions

1. In a large pan, melt the butter on medium heat and sauté the leeks for about 15 minutes.
2. In a bowl, mix together the cornstarch and broth.
3. In the pan, add the potatoes and broth mixture and bring to a boil.
4. Season with the salt and pepper.
5. Stir in the cream and reduce the heat.
6. Simmer for about 30 minutes.
7. Season with the salt and pepper before serving.

All You Need is Thyme Potato Soup

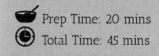 Prep Time: 20 mins

Total Time: 45 mins

Servings per Recipe: 6

Calories	338 kcal
Fat	10.8 g
Carbohydrates	51.6g
Protein	10.1 g
Cholesterol	31 mg
Sodium	857 mg

Ingredients

1/4 C. butter
1 large onion, chopped
6 potatoes, peeled and diced
2 carrots, diced
3 C. water
2 tbsp chicken bouillon powder
ground black pepper to taste

3 tbsp all-purpose flour
3 C. milk
1 tbsp dried parsley
1/4 tsp dried thyme

Directions

1. In a pan, melt the butter on medium heat and sauté the onion for about 5 minutes.
2. Meanwhile in another pan, add the potatoes, carrots, water and chicken soup base and bring to a boil.
3. Cook for about 10 minutes.
4. Season with the ground black pepper to taste.
5. Add the flour, stirring continuously till smooth.
6. Cook, stirring continuously for about 2 minutes.
7. Slowly, add the milk and stir well.
8. Reduce the heat to low heat and cook, stirring continuously till warmed completely.
9. Add the potato and carrot mixture, parsley and thyme and cook till heated completely.
10. Serve hot.

SWISS STYLE
Potato Soup

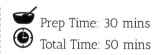

Prep Time: 30 mins
Total Time: 50 mins

Servings per Recipe: 6

Calories	311 kcal
Fat	13.1 g
Carbohydrates	37.1g
Protein	12.1 g
Cholesterol	40 mg
Sodium	638 mg

Ingredients

4 potatoes, peeled and quartered
1 small carrot, finely chopped
1/2 stalk celery, finely chopped
1 small onion, minced
1 1/2 C. vegetable broth
1 tsp salt

2 1/2 C. milk
3 tbsp butter, melted
3 tbsp all-purpose flour
1 tbsp dried parsley
1 tsp ground black pepper
1 C. shredded Swiss cheese

Directions

1. In a large pan, add the potatoes, carrots, celery, onion, vegetable broth and salt and bring to a boil.
2. Reduce the heat and simmer, covered till the potatoes become just tender.
3. With a potato masher, mash the mixture slightly and stir in the milk.
4. In a small bowl, add the butter, flour, parsley and pepper and beat to combine.
5. Add the butter mixture into the potato mixture.
6. Cook and stir on the medium heat till the mixture becomes thick and bubbly.
7. Remove from the heat and immediately, stir in the cheese and stir till the cheese is almost melted.
8. Keep aside the soup for about 5 minutes.

Potato Soup
Summers

🥣 Prep Time: 30 mins
🕐 Total Time: 1 hr 10 mins

Servings per Recipe: 16
Calories	321 kcal
Fat	9.4 g
Carbohydrates	39.6g
Protein	19.9 g
Cholesterol	42 mg
Sodium	1294 mg

Ingredients

12 potatoes, peeled and cubed
2 large onions, finely chopped
2 lb. processed cheese food
1 lb. chopped turkey, optional
ground black pepper to taste
3 1/2 tbsp all-purpose flour
1 C. milk

Directions

1. In a large soup pan, mix together the potatoes, onion, and cubed turkey.
2. Add enough water and cook till the potatoes becomes almost tender.
3. In a bowl, add about 1 C. of the cooked potatoes and with a fork, mash them.
4. Add some of the liquid from the pan and in a bowl with the flour and mix till a thick paste form.
5. Add the flour paste in the soup and stir to combine.
6. Place the cubed cheese in the pan and simmer till the cheese melts completely.
7. Add ground black pepper to taste and stir in the milk.

PEANUT
Potato Soup

Prep Time: 30 mins
Total Time: 50 mins

Servings per Recipe: 8	
Calories	207 kcal
Fat	9 g
Carbohydrates	28.7g
Protein	5 g
Cholesterol	11 mg
Sodium	462 mg

Ingredients

1/2 C. sour cream
1 tsp grated lime zest
2 large sweet potatoes, peeled and cubed
1 tbsp butter
1 onion, sliced
2 cloves garlic, sliced
4 C. chicken stock
1/2 tsp ground cumin

1/4 tsp crushed red pepper flakes
2 tbsp grated fresh ginger root
1/4 C. smooth peanut butter
1 lime, juiced
2 tbsp chopped fresh cilantro
salt to taste
1 large roma (plum) tomato, seeded and diced

Directions

1. In a small bowl, mix together the sour cream and lime zest and refrigerate to allow the flavors to blend.
2. In a large pan, melt the butter on medium heat and sauté the onion and garlic for about 5 minutes.
3. Add the sweet potatoes, chicken broth, cumin, chili flakes and ginger and bring to a boil.
4. Reduce the heat to low, and simmer, covered for about 15 minutes.
5. With an immersion blender, puree the soup.
6. Add the peanut butter into the soup, beating continuously till well combined.
7. Simmer till heated completely.
8. Stir in the lime juice and salt.
9. Place the soup into the warm bowls and top with a dollop of the reserved sour cream, a few pieces of the diced tomato and a sprinkle of the cilantro.

Cream of Chicken Potato Soup

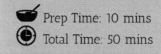

Prep Time: 10 mins
Total Time: 50 mins

Servings per Recipe: 6	
Calories	404 kcal
Fat	24.8 g
Carbohydrates	32.9 g
Protein	12.5 g
Cholesterol	42 mg
Sodium	1026 mg

Ingredients

8 slices turkey bacon, optional
1 C. chopped onion
4 C. cubed potatoes
2 (10.75 oz.) cans condensed cream of chicken soup
2 1/2 C. milk
salt to taste
ground black pepper to taste
1 tsp dried dill weed

Directions

1. Heat a large pan and cook the bacon till browned completely.
2. Transfer the bacon onto a paper towel lined plate to drain and then crumble it.
3. Discard the bacon grease, leaving about 3 tbsp inside the pan.
4. Heat the bacon grease on medium heat and cook the onion till browned.
5. Add the potatoes and enough water to cover.
6. Cook, covered for about 15-20 minutes.
7. In a bowl, add the cream of chicken soup and milk and mix till smooth.
8. Add the milk mixture into the soup mixture and cool till just heated.
9. Stir in the salt, pepper and dill weed and remove from the heat.
10. Serve the soup with a topping of the bacon.

CREAM
of Mushroom
Potato Soup

 Prep Time: 30 mins

Total Time: 50 mins

Servings per Recipe: 9

Calories	642 kcal
Fat	38.9 g
Carbohydrates	41.2g
Protein	31.8 g
Cholesterol	105 mg
Sodium	2352 mg

Ingredients

8 unpeeled potatoes, cubed
1 onion, chopped
2 stalks celery, diced
6 cubes chicken bouillon
1 pint half-and-half cream
1 lb. turkey bacon - cooked and

crumbled, optional
1 (10.75 oz.) can condensed cream of
mushroom soup
2 C. shredded Cheddar cheese

Directions

1. In a large soup pan mix together the potatoes, onions, celery, bouillon cubes and enough water to cover the all ingredients and bring to a boil on medium heat.
2. Simmer for about 15 minutes.
3. Add the half and half, bacon and cream of mushroom soup and stir till smooth and creamy.
4. Add the cheese and stir till melts completely.
5. Simmer on low heat till the potatoes are cooked through.

Perfect
Autumn Soup

Prep Time: 35 mins

Total Time: 1 hr 5 mins

Servings per Recipe: 4

Calories	286 kcal
Fat	6.3 g
Carbohydrates	53.7g
Protein	4.9 g
Cholesterol	18 mg
Sodium	765 mg

Ingredients

2 tbsp butter
1 onion, diced
1/2 tsp ground cardamom
1/4 tsp ground turmeric
1/4 tsp ground ginger
1/4 tsp red pepper flakes
1/4 tsp ground cinnamon

1 pinch cayenne pepper
1 (14 oz.) can chicken broth
2 C. water
2 large sweet potatoes, peeled and diced
3 carrots, peeled and chopped
Salt and pepper to taste

Directions

1. In a large pan, melt the butter on medium-high heat and sauté the onion for about 5-7 minutes.
2. Stir in the cardamom, turmeric, ginger, pepper flakes, cinnamon and cayenne and sauté for about 1 minute.
3. Add the chicken broth, water, sweet potatoes and carrots and bring to a boil on high heat.
4. Reduce the heat to medium-low and simmer, covered for about 25-30 minutes.
5. Remove from the heat and keep aside to cool slightly.
6. In a blender, add the soup in batches and pulse till smooth.

ANTI-INFLAMMATORY
Potato Soup

Prep Time: 30 mins
Total Time: 1 hr 2 mins

Servings per Recipe: 4

Calories	388 kcal
Fat	12.6 g
Carbohydrates	59.8g
Protein	9.6 g
Cholesterol	35 mg
Sodium	587 mg

Ingredients

6 oz. egg noodles
3 tbsp extra-virgin olive oil
1 (2 inch) piece ginger root, minced
2 cloves garlic, minced
1 leek, sliced into 1/2-inch pieces
2 carrots, cut into cubes
2 stalks celery, sliced into 1/2-inch

pieces
2 potatoes, peeled and cubed
1 tsp turmeric powder
1/2 tsp ground white pepper
1/2 tsp salt
3 C. water
2 C. vegetable broth

Directions

1. In large pan of the lightly salted boiling water, cook the egg noodles for about 3 minutes.
2. Drain well.
3. In a large pan, heat the oil on medium heat and sauté the garlic and ginger for about 1 minute.
4. Stir in the leeks and cook for about 3 minutes.
5. Stir in the carrots and celery and cook for about 2 minutes.
6. Stir in the potatoes and cook for about 2 minutes.
7. Cook, covered for about 5 minutes.
8. Stir in the turmeric, white pepper, salt and water and bring to a boil.
9. In another pan, add the vegetable broth and bring to a boil.
10. Remove from the heat and stir in the potato soup mixture.
11. Stir in the egg noodles and simmer for about 5 minutes.

Shallots and Carrots Potato Soup

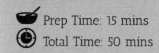 Prep Time: 15 mins

Total Time: 50 mins

Servings per Recipe: 5

Calories	131 kcal
Fat	2.1 g
Carbohydrates	23.1g
Protein	5.7 g
Cholesterol	0 mg
Sodium	539 mg

Ingredients

2 tsp canola oil
1/2 C. chopped shallots
3 C. 1/2-inch cubes peeled sweet potato
1 1/2 C. 1/4-inch slices peeled carrot
1 tbsp grated fresh ginger root
2 tsp curry powder
3 C. fat free, low-sodium chicken broth

1/2 tsp salt

Directions

1. In a large pan, heat the oil on medium-high heat and sauté the shallots for about 3 minutes.
2. Stir in the sweet potato, carrot, ginger and curry powder and cook for about 3-4 minutes.
3. Add the chicken broth and bring to a boil.
4. Reduce the heat to low and simmer, covered for about 25-30 minutes.
5. Season the soup with the salt.
6. Remove from the heat and keep aside to cool slightly.
7. In a blender, add the soup in batches and pulse till smooth.

A VEGAN'S
Potato Soup

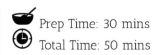

Prep Time: 30 mins
Total Time: 50 mins

Servings per Recipe: 6

Calories	161 kcal
Fat	3.1 g
Carbohydrates	31.3g
Protein	3.8 g
Cholesterol	1 mg
Sodium	1196 mg

Ingredients

4 large carrots, thinly sliced
2 large potatoes, thinly sliced
1 large onion, thinly sliced
1/4 medium head green cabbage, thinly sliced
2 cloves garlic, smashed

6 C. chicken stock
1 tbsp olive oil
1/4 tsp dried thyme
1/4 tsp dried basil
1 tsp dried parsley
1 tsp salt
ground black pepper to taste

Directions

1. In a large soup pan, mix together the carrots, potatoes, onion, cabbage, garlic, chicken broth, olive oil, thyme, basil, parsley, salt and pepper on medium-high heat and bring to a boil.
2. Cook for about 20 minutes.
3. Remove from the heat and keep aside to cool slightly.
4. In a blender, add the soup in batches and pulse till smooth.

Beef Based
Corn Potato Soup

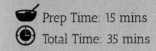 Prep Time: 15 mins

Total Time: 35 mins

Servings per Recipe: 8
Calories	156 kcal
Fat	3.7 g
Carbohydrates	29g
Protein	4.1 g
Cholesterol	8 mg
Sodium	848 mg

Ingredients

4 potatoes, peeled and quartered
1 (14 oz.) can whole kernel corn
1/2 C. chopped onion
2 tbsp butter
1 tbsp beef base
1 tsp salt
1/4 tsp red pepper flakes

1/8 tsp ground black pepper
water, as needed

Directions

1. In a large pan, mix together the potatoes, corn, onion, butter, beef base, salt, red pepper flakes, black pepper and enough water over the mixture to cover by 2 inches and bring to a boil.
2. Reduce the heat to medium-low and simmer for about 20 minutes.
3. Remove from the heat and keep aside to cool slightly.
4. In a blender, add the soup in batches and pulse till smooth.

SHRIMP AND LEEKS
Potato Soup

Prep Time: 35 mins
Total Time: 6 hr 35 mins

Servings per Recipe: 6	
Calories	284 kcal
Fat	7.5 g
Carbohydrates	39.8g
Protein	15.7 g
Cholesterol	80 mg
Sodium	950 mg

Ingredients

4 thick slices turkey bacon, diced, optional
1 tbsp butter, optional
3 leeks, thinly sliced (white and pale green parts only)
2 stalks celery, chopped
2 cloves garlic, minced
4 red potatoes, cut into 1-inch pieces
4 C. chicken broth
2 C. water
1/2 tsp dried thyme

1/2 tsp ground paprika
1 pinch cayenne pepper
salt and ground black pepper to taste
3 sprigs fresh thyme
1 C. frozen sweet corn
1/2 C. milk
18 large tiger shrimp
2 tbsp cornstarch
1 tbsp water
1 tbsp chopped fresh parsley

Directions

1. Heat a large skillet on medium heat and cook the bacon for about 10 minutes.
2. Transfer the bacon onto a paper towel lined plate to drain.
3. Discard the bacon grease from the skillet, leaving just 1 tbsp.
4. Heat the butter on medium heat and sauté the leeks and celery for about 5 minutes.
5. Stir in the garlic and sauté for about 2 minutes.
6. Transfer the leek mixture into a slow cooker.
7. Add the cooked bacon, potatoes, chicken broth, 2 C. of the water, dried thyme, paprika, cayenne pepper, salt and black pepper.
8. With the kitchen strings, tie the thyme sprigs and place into the slow cooker.
9. Set the slow cooker on High and cook, covered for about 4 hours.
10. Stir in the corn and cook for about 1 hour more.
11. Now, set the slow cooker on Low.
12. Stir in the milk and cook, uncovered for about 30-40 minutes.

13. Meanwhile, in a pan, add the water and bring to a boil.
14. Add the tiger shrimp in the boiling water and cook for about 3 minutes.
15. Drain well and keep aside to cool slightly before peeling.
16. In a bowl, mix together the cornstarch and 1 tbsp of the water.
17. Add the cornstarch mixture into the slow cooker, stirring continuously.
18. Cook the soup for about 3 minutes more.
19. Stir in the peeled shrimp and parsley.
20. Discard the fresh thyme sprigs and season the soup with the salt and black pepper before serving.

POTLUCK
Potato Soup

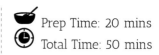 Prep Time: 20 mins
Total Time: 50 mins

Servings per Recipe: 8
Calories	359 kcal
Fat	19.7 g
Carbohydrates	34.4g
Protein	14.8 g
Cholesterol	57 mg
Sodium	901 mg

Ingredients

2 C. peeled and diced potatoes
1/2 C. diced carrots
1/2 C. diced celery
1/4 C. chopped onion
1 tsp salt
1/4 C. butter

2 C. milk
1/4 C. all-purpose flour
2 (15 oz.) cans whole kernel corn, drained
2 1/2 C. shredded Cheddar cheese

Directions

1. In a large pan, add the potatoes, carrots, celery, onion, salt and enough water to cover the mixture and bring to a boil.
2. Reduce the heat and simmer for about 20 minutes.
3. Meanwhile, in a small pan, mix together the butter, milk and flour on medium-low heat.
4. Cook, stirring continuously till the mixture becomes thick and smooth.
5. Add the milk mixture into the soup and stir to combine.
6. Stir in the corn and cheese and cook till the cheese melts completely.
7. Serve immediately.

Hash Brown
Gravy Potato Soup

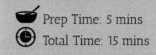

Prep Time: 5 mins
Total Time: 15 mins

Servings per Recipe: 6

Calories	135 kcal
Fat	1.7 g
Carbohydrates	21.4g
Protein	9.5 g
Cholesterol	5 mg
Sodium	924 mg

Ingredients

1 (16 oz.) package frozen loose-pack hash brown potatoes with onion and peppers
2 (10.5 oz.) cans fat-free chicken broth
1 (2.5 oz.) package fat free country-style gravy mix
1/2 C. water
1/2 C. chopped green onion for topping

1 C. shredded reduced-fat Cheddar cheese

Directions

1. In a soup pan mix together the hash browns and chicken broth and bring to a boil.
2. Reduce the heat to medium-low and simmer for about 10 minutes.
3. In a bowl, mix together the gravy mix and water.
4. Add the gravy mixture into the soup and simmer till the mixture becomes thick.
5. Remove from the heat and keep aside for a few minutes before serving.
6. Serve hot with a garnishing of the chopped green onions and grated cheese.

5-INGREDIENT
Potato Soup

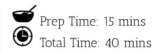 Prep Time: 15 mins
Total Time: 40 mins

Servings per Recipe: 4
Calories	519 kcal
Fat	26 g
Carbohydrates	56.2g
Protein	17.3 g
Cholesterol	85 mg
Sodium	215 mg

Ingredients

4 potatoes, peeled and cubed
water to cover
2 (12 fluid oz.) cans evaporated milk
4 tbsp unsalted butter
salt and pepper to taste

Directions

1. In a large pan, mix together the potatoes on high heat.
2. Add enough water to cover, about 1 inch over the potatoes and bring to a boil.
3. Cook for about 10-15 minutes.
4. Reduce the heat to low and stir in the evaporated milk and butter.
5. With a potato masher, mash the potatoes.
6. Season with the salt and white pepper to taste.

Lick-the-Bowl
Potato Soup

🥣 Prep Time: 10 mins
🕐 Total Time: 30 mins

Servings per Recipe: 4
Calories	174 kcal
Fat	8.4 g
Carbohydrates	17.8g
Protein	7.2 g
Cholesterol	18 mg
Sodium	616 mg

Ingredients

2 C. broccoli florets
1 onion, sliced
1 tbsp margarine
1 (10.75 oz.) can condensed cream of potato soup
1 C. milk
1/2 C. water

3/4 tsp chopped fresh basil
1/4 tsp ground black pepper
1/3 C. shredded Cheddar cheese

Directions

1. In a large pan, melt the margarine on medium heat and sauté the broccoli and onion for about 5 minutes.
2. Stir in the soup, milk, water, basil and pepper and cook for about 15 minutes.
3. Add the cheese and stir till melted completely.

NO-FUSS
Potato Soup

Prep Time: 20 mins
Total Time: 8 hr 20 mins

Servings per Recipe: 8
Calories	218 kcal
Fat	9.3 g
Carbohydrates	26.4g
Protein	8.2 g
Cholesterol	27 mg
Sodium	342 mg

Ingredients

5 potatoes, diced
1 C. diced fully cooked turkey
2/3 C. finely chopped leek
1/3 C. diced celery
1/3 C. diced carrots
1/4 C. butter

1 tbsp garlic powder
1 tsp dill
1 bay leaf
salt to taste
coarsely ground black pepper to taste
48 fluid oz. low-sodium chicken broth

Directions

1. In a slow cooker, mix together the potatoes, turkey, leek, celery, carrots, butter, garlic powder, dill, bay leaf, salt and pepper.
2. Place the chicken broth over the potato mixture.
3. Set the slow cooker on Low and cook, covered for about 8 hours.

Louisiana
Crawfish Red Potato Soup

🍲 Prep Time: 15 mins
🕐 Total Time: 1 hr

Servings per Recipe: 12

Calories	250 kcal
Fat	14.5 g
Carbohydrates	17.2g
Protein	13.4 g
Cholesterol	85 mg
Sodium	198 mg

Ingredients

3 slices turkey bacon
1 onion, chopped
1 green bell pepper, seeded and chopped
1 red bell pepper, seeded and chopped
2 stalks celery, finely chopped
2 tbsp minced garlic
5 C. diced red potatoes

1 C. grated carrot
1 lb. crawfish tails
3 C. chicken broth
1 quart half-and-half cream
salt and pepper to taste
1 C. shredded Cheddar cheese

Directions

1. Heat a large pan on medium-high heat and cook the bacon till browned completely.
2. Transfer the bacon onto a paper towel lined plate to drain and then crumble it.
3. Return the bacon into the pan and reduce the heat to medium.
4. Add the onion, green pepper, red pepper, celery and garlic and sauté till the onion and peppers become tender.
5. Stir in the crawfish and cook till all the liquid evaporates and the crawfish begin to brown.
6. Transfer the crawfish mixture into a bowl and keep aside.
7. In the same pan, add the chicken broth and potatoes and bring to a boil.
8. Cook for about 8-10 minutes.
9. Stir in the carrots and cook for about 8 minutes.
10. Reduce the heat to low and return the crawfish mixture into the pan.
11. Stir in the half-and-half and cook till heated completely.
12. Season with the salt and pepper.
13. Place the soup into the bowls and serve with a topping of the Cheddar cheese.

FRIED
Ramen Rings

🥣 Prep Time: 20 mins
🕐 Total Time: 35 mins

Servings per Recipe: 1
Calories	1490.7
Fat	37.4g
Cholesterol	372.0mg
Sodium	7533.7mg
Carbohydrates	224.1g
Protein	45.5g

Ingredients
Batter for Frying, reserve 2 C.
1 C. self-rising flour
1 tsp salt
1/4 tsp pepper
2 eggs, beaten
1 C. beer, or milk
Onions

2 (3 oz.) packages ramen noodles, packet reserved
oil, for frying
1 large Vidalia onion, ringed

Directions
1. Get a large mixing bowl: Whisk in it the flour, eggs, beer, a pinch of salt and pepper.
2. Get a food processor: Cut the one ramen in half and process it in it until it becomes ground. Add it to the flour batter and mix them well.
3. Finely crush the other ramen and place it in a shallow dish. Add to it the seasoning packet and mix them well.
4. Place a large pan over medium heat. Fill 3/4 inch of it with oil and heat it.
5. Coat the onion rings with the flour batter and dip them in the crushed noodles mix. Place them in the hot oil and cook them until they become golden brown.
6. Serve your onion rings with your favorite dip.
7. Enjoy.

Mock
Ramen Pot Pie

🥣 Prep Time: 15 mins
🕐 Total Time: 30 mins

Servings per Recipe: 4
Calories   528.6
Fat   24.9 g
Cholesterol   77.1mg
Sodium   957.3mg
Carbohydrates   49.0 g
Protein   29.1g

Ingredients

2 (3 oz.) packages ramen noodles
1 lb ground beef
1 (15 oz.) cans sweet corn
1/2 C. onion, chopped
vegetable oil

Directions

1. Before you do anything preheat the oven to 350 F.
2. Prepare the noodles according to the directions on the package.
3. Place a large pan over medium heat. Heat a splash of oil in it. Cook in it the beef with onion for 12 min.
4. Spread the mix in the bottom of a greased baking pan. Top it with the sweet corn and the ramen noodles after draining it.
5. Place the casserole in the oven and cook it for 14 to 16 min. Serve it warm.
6. Enjoy.

TROPICAL
Curry Ramen

🥣 Prep Time: 20 mins
🕐 Total Time: 30 mins

Servings per Recipe: 4	
Calories	553.2
Fat	25.4g
Cholesterol	0.0mg
Sodium	1466.3mg
Carbohydrates	76.3g
Protein	8.5g

Ingredients

2 (3 oz.) packages ramen noodles
1 tbsp vegetable oil
1 tsp crushed red pepper flakes
2 garlic cloves, minced
1 C. shredded cabbage
1 C. thinly sliced mixed mushrooms
1 C. chopped broccoli
1 tbsp peanut butter
1 tbsp soy sauce

1 tbsp brown sugar
1 C. coconut milk
1 tsp curry powder
1 tsp sambal oelek
1 lime, juice of
1/2 tsp salt
1 tbsp crushed peanuts
1/4 C. chopped cilantro
lime wedge

Directions

1. Prepare the noodles according to the directions on the package without the seasoning packets. Drain the noodles and reserve the cooking liquid.

2. Place a large pan over medium heat. Heat the oil in it. Sauté in it the garlic with red pepper for 40 sec.

3. Stir in the cabbage, mushrooms and broccoli. Add the veggies and cook them for 6 min. Stir the noodles into the pan and place them aside.

4. Place another pan over medium heat. Stir in it the peanut butter, soy sauce, brown sugar, coconut milk, curry powder, sambal oelek and salt. Cook them until they start boiling.

5. Add the cooked noodles and veggies and stir them to coat. Stir in 1/4 C. of the cooking liquid. Cook them until they mix becomes thick.

6. Let the ramen skillet rest for 6 min. Top the ramen skillet with the cilantro and peanuts then serve them hot.

7. Enjoy.

Golden Cheddar Ramen Soup

Prep Time: 2 mins
Total Time: 8 mins

Servings per Recipe: 1
Calories   617.0
Fat   24.4g
Cholesterol   30.6mg
Sodium   1236.9mg
Carbohydrates   85.0g
Protein   17.2g

Ingredients

Ramen
1 (3 oz.) packages ramen noodles
2 C. water
Base
1 seasoning, packet
1-2 C. water

1 tbsp freshly shredded parmesan cheese
1/4 C. shredded aged white cheddar cheese
1/4 C. golden raisins
Tabasco sauce

Directions

1. Stir 2 C. of water and 1 ramen packet in a heatproof bowl. Place it in the microwave for 5 to 7 min.
2. Once the time is up, stir the parmesan and cheddar cheese into the noodles until they melt. Fold the raisins into it and serve it hot.
3. Enjoy.

HOT SHOT
of Ramen

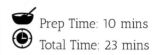

Prep Time: 10 mins
Total Time: 23 mins

Servings per Recipe: 2
Calories   365.6
Fat   15.5g
Cholesterol   47.5mg
Sodium   861.7mg
Carbohydrates   35.0g
Protein   20.8g

Ingredients
1 1/2 C. water
1 small yellow onion, finely diced
1 celery rib, finely diced
6 baby carrots, julienne
1 (3 oz.) packages ramen noodles, broken
1 (5 1/2 oz.) cans sardines in tomato sauce
2-3 dashes hot sauce

Directions
1. Place a large saucepan of water over medium heat. Stir in it the water, onion, celery, and carrots. Cook them for 12 min.
2. Stir in the noodles and cook it for 3 to 4 min.
3. Stir the sardines with tomato, and hot sauce into the saucepan. Serve it hot with your favorite toppings.
4. Enjoy.

4-Ingredient
Ramen

Prep Time: 5 mins
Total Time: 10 mins

Servings per Recipe: 2
Calories	306.7
Fat	19.2g
Cholesterol	34.8mg
Sodium	989.2mg
Carbohydrates	28.4g
Protein	5.5g

Ingredients

1 (3 oz.) packages ramen noodles, any
flavor
2 C. water
2 tbsp butter
1/4 C. milk

Directions

1. Place a pot over medium heat and fill most of it with water. Cook it until it starts boiling.
2. Stir in it the noodles and let it cook for 4 min. discard the water and place the noodles in an empty pot.
3. Stir in it the milk with butter and seasoning mix. Cook them for 3 to 5 min over low heat until they become creamy. Serve it warm.
4. Enjoy.

MUNG BANG
Noodles Skillet

Prep Time: 45 mins
Total Time: 1 hr

Servings per Recipe: 6

Calories	378.5
Fat	16.0g
Cholesterol	54.5mg
Sodium	1082.0mg
Carbohydrates	36.5g
Protein	23.9g

Ingredients

1 lb lean ground beef, cooked
6 slices turkey bacon, chopped
2 (3 oz.) packages ramen noodles
3 garlic cloves, minced
1 medium red onion, diced
1 medium cabbage, chopped
3 carrots, cut into thin 1 inch strips

1 red bell pepper, cut into bite size pieces
2-4 tbsp light soy sauce
3 C. bean sprouts
light soy sauce, to taste
crushed red pepper flakes

Directions

1. Place a large pan over medium heat.
2. Cook in it the bacon until it becomes crisp. Drain it and place it aside. Keep about 2 tbsp of the bacon grease in the pan.
3. Sauté in it the garlic with onion for 4 min. Stir in 2 tbsp of soy sauce and the carrots.
4. Let them cook for 3 min. Stir in the bell pepper with cabbage and let them cook for an extra 7 min.
5. Cook the noodles according to the manufacturer's directions. Drain it and stir it with a splash of olive oil.
6. Stir the beef, bacon and crushed red pepper flakes into the skillet with the cooked veggies. Let them cook for 4 min while stirring often.
7. Once the time is up, stir the bean sprouts and Ramen noodles into the veggies mix. Let them cook for an extra 3 min while stirring all the time.
8. Serve your noodles skillet warm with some hot sauce.
9. Enjoy.

French
Ramen Pan

🥣 Prep Time: 20 mins

🕐 Total Time: 50 mins

Servings per Recipe: 1	
Calories	540.8
Fat	29.1g
Cholesterol	61.2mg
Sodium	1928.8mg
Carbohydrates	45.9g
Protein	23.2g

Ingredients

2 (3 oz.) packages ramen noodles, any flavor
2 tbsp sour cream
1 (10 1/2 oz.) cans cream of mushroom soup
1/2 C. water

1/2 C. milk
1/4 C. onion, chopped
1/4 C. French's French fried onions
1/2 lb ground beef

Directions

1. Before you do anything, preheat the oven to 375 F.
2. Get a mixing bowl: Stir in it the crusted noodles, 1 packet of seasoning, sour cream, soup (undiluted) water, milk, and onion.
3. Place a large pan over medium heat. Cook in it the beef for 8 min. Drain it and add it to the noodles mix. Stir them to coat.
4. Pour the mix into a greased pan. Cook it in the oven for 22 min.
5. Top the noodles pan with the fried onion and cook it for an extra 12 min in the oven.
6. Top it with the cheese then serve it warm.
7. Enjoy.

SWEET RAMEN
Skillet

🥣 Prep Time: 10 mins
🕐 Total Time: 30 mins

Servings per Recipe: 6
Calories	334.3
Fat	11.6g
Cholesterol	48.6mg
Sodium	703.7mg
Carbohydrates	38.0g
Protein	19.9g

Ingredients
1 C. bell pepper, chopped
1/2 tsp ginger
4 whole green onions, thinly sliced
1 (20 oz.) cans pineapple, undrained
1 lb boneless chicken breast
oil
2 (3 oz.) packages chicken-flavored ramen
noodles
1/2 C. sweet and sour sauce

Directions
1. Pour the pineapple juice in a measuring C. Stir in it enough water to make 2 C. of liquid in total.
2. Slice the chicken breast into 1 inch dices. Sprinkle over them ginger, a pinch of salt and pepper.
3. Place a large pan over medium heat. Heat a splash of oil in it. Stir in the ramen's seasoning packets and cook them for 30 sec.
4. Stir the pineapple liquid mix into the pan with noodles after cutting into pieces.
5. Cook the mix until it starts boiling. Lower the heat and cook them for 4 min.
6. Once the time is up, stir sweet and sour sauce, pepper, onion, and pineapple into the pan. Let them cook for 4 to 6 min or until the veggies are done.
7. Serve your sweet ramen skillet warm.
8. Enjoy.

How to Make
Miso Ramen

🥣 Prep Time: 5 mins
🕐 Total Time: 20 mins

Servings per Recipe: 5
Calories	279.8
Fat	12.0g
Cholesterol	8.1mg
Sodium	1397.2mg
Carbohydrates	32.7g
Protein	12.4g

Ingredients

2 tsp olive oil
1 garlic clove, minced
1 tsp fresh ginger, minced
2-4 oz. ground turkey
5 oz. bean sprouts, rinsed
4 oz. cabbage, chopped
2-4 oz. carrots, cut into thin strips

4 C. low sodium chicken broth
1 tsp sugar
2 tsp light soy sauce
4 tbsp miso
2 (3 oz.) packages ramen noodles
1/2 tsp sesame oil

Directions

1. Place a large saucepan over medium heat. Heat the oil in it. sauté in it the garlic with ginger and turkey for 8 min until done.
2. Stir in the carrots, bean sprouts and cabbage and cook them for 4 min.
3. Stir in the broth with soy sauce and sugar. Cook them until they start boiling.
4. Turn the heat down and sit the miso into the soup with the sesame oil.
5. Enjoy.

MARINATED
Eggs for Ramen

Prep Time: 5 mins
Total Time: 10 mins

Servings per Recipe: 1

Calories	83.1
Fat	5.3g
Cholesterol	211.5mg
Sodium	405.1mg
Carbohydrates	1.4g
Protein	6.9g

Ingredients
6 eggs
1 tbsp rice vinegar
2 tbsp soy sauce
1 tsp sugar
1/2 tsp sesame oil

Directions
1. Place a pot over medium heat. Place in it the eggs and cover them with water. Cook them until they start boiling.
2. Turn off the heat and put on the lid. Let the eggs sit for 10 min.
3. Once the time is up drain the eggs and place them in a bowl. Cover them with some cold water and let them sit for 6 min. Peel them and place them aside.
4. Get a small heavy saucepan: Whisk in it the vinegar, soy sauce, sugar, and sesame oil to make the marinade.
5. Cook them over medium heat until they start boiling. Turn off the heat and place the marinade aside until it becomes warm.
6. Place the eggs in a large mason jar and pour the marinade all over them. Seal it and place it aside to sit for 1 day.
7. Once the time is up, drain the eggs and serve them with your ramen.
8. Enjoy.

Apple
Ramen Salad

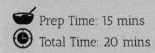 Prep Time: 15 mins
🕐 Total Time: 20 mins

Servings per Recipe: 10
Calories	343.1
Fat	28.5g
Cholesterol	9.1mg
Sodium	235.0mg
Carbohydrates	19.8g
Protein	4.0g

Ingredients

12 oz. broccoli florets
1 (12 oz.) bags broccoli coleslaw mix
1/4 C. sunflower seeds
2 (3 oz.) packages ramen noodles
3 tbsp butter
2 tbsp olive oil
1/4 C. sliced almonds

3/4 C. vegetable oil
1/4 C. brown sugar
1/4 C. apple cider vinegar
1/4 C. green onion, chopped

Directions

1. Place a large skillet over medium heat. Heat the oil in it.
2. Press your ramen with your hands to crush it. Stir it in the pan with the almonds.
3. Cook them for 6 min then place the skillet aside.
4. Get a large mixing bowl: Toss in it the broccoli, broccoli slaw and sunflowers. Add the noodles mix and toss them again.
5. Get a small mixing bowl: Combine in it the vegetable oil, brown sugar, apple cider vinegar and the Ramen noodle seasoning packet to make the vinaigrette.
6. Drizzle the vinaigrette all over the salad and stir it to coat. Serve your salad with the green onions on top.
7. Enjoy.

RAMEN
Omelet

Prep Time: 10 mins

Total Time: 25 mins

Servings per Recipe: 6	
Calories	247.9
Fat	12.2g
Cholesterol	218.8mg
Sodium	534.9mg
Carbohydrates	21.6g
Protein	12.4g

Ingredients
2 (3 oz.) packages ramen noodles, cooked
according to directions
6 eggs
1 red bell pepper, chopped
1 large carrot, grated
1/2 C. parmesan cheese, grated

Directions
1. Get a mixing bowl: Mix in it the eggs with 1 ramen seasoning packet.
2. Add the noodles, bell pepper and carrot. Mix them well.
3. Before you do anything else, preheat the oven to 356 F.
4. Grease a muffin tin with some butter or a cooking spray. Spoon the batter into the tins. Top the muffins with the parmesan cheese.
5. Cook the muffins in the oven for 16 min. Serve them warm.
6. Enjoy.

Ramen
Seoul

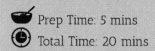 Prep Time: 5 mins

Total Time: 20 mins

Servings per Recipe: 2
Calories	303.0
Fat	9.1g14%
Cholesterol	93.0mg
Sodium	907.1mg
Carbohydrates	45.7g
Protein	9.7g

Ingredients
1 medium potato
1 package ramen noodles
1 green onion, sliced (optional)
1 large egg, beaten

Directions
1. Discard the potato skin and slice them into small dices.
2. Prepare the noodles according to the directions on the package while adding the potato to it and adding 1/4 of the water needed to the pot.
3. Stir the seasoning packet and cook them for potato until it becomes soft.
4. Combine the green onion into the pot and cook them until the ramen is done. Add the eggs to the soup while stirring all the time until they are cooked.
5. Serve your soup hot.
6. Enjoy.

RAMEN
Toscano

Prep Time: 25 mins
Total Time: 60 mins

Servings per Recipe: 4
Calories	611.7
Fat	36.9g
Cholesterol	233.6mg
Sodium	1256.4mg
Carbohydrates	51.4g
Protein	20.2g

Ingredients

1/4 C. olive oil
3 (3 oz.) packages ramen noodles, packet removed
1/2 red bell pepper, sliced
1/4 red onion, sliced
1 small carrot, thinly sliced
3 C. broccoli florets
2 tsp garlic, minced
1 tsp basil
4 eggs, beaten
Spice Mix
1/2 C. parmesan cheese, grated

1/2 C. half-and-half cream
1 tbsp oregano
1/2 tsp kosher salt
3/4 tsp paprika
1/4 tsp dry mustard
3/4 tsp ground fennel
3/4 tsp granulated garlic
3/4 tsp granulated onion
1/4 tsp cayenne pepper
1 pinch sugar

Directions

1. Before you do anything, preheat the oven to 400 F.
2. Get a large mixing bowl: Stir in it the seasoning mix with 1/4 C. of olive oil. Toss the red bell pepper, red onion, broccoli florets into the mix.
3. Stir 1 tsp of minced garlic and basil.
4. Before you do anything, preheat the oven to 350 F.
5. Pour the veggies mix into a greased baking sheet. Cook it in the oven for 22 min.
6. Heat 4 quarts of water in a large pot over medium heat. Cook in it the ramen noodles for 3 to 4 min. Remove the noodles from the water.
7. Get a large mixing bowl: Combine in it the beaten egg, minced garlic, grated Parmesan cheese. Add the noodles and toss them to coat with a pinch of salt and pepper.
8. Grease a casserole dish with some butter. Pour the noodles mix in it and spread it in the pan to make the crust.
9. Spread the baked veggies over the ramen crust.
10. Get a small mixing bowl: Combine in it 3 eggs, the remaining 1/4 C. Parmesan cheese, and 1/2 C. of half and half cream. Mix them well.
11. Drizzle the mix all over the veggies. Cover the pie with a piece of foil. Cook it in the oven for 22 min.
12. Once the time is up, discard the foil. Sprinkle the remaining cheese on top and cook the pie for an extra 12 min.
13. Serve it warm.
14. Enjoy.

Sambal
Ramen Salad

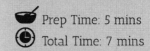 Prep Time: 5 mins

Total Time: 7 mins

Servings per Recipe: 2	
Calories	425.7
Fat	23.8g
Cholesterol	5.7mg
Sodium	706.6mg
Carbohydrates	46.2g
Protein	10.4g

Ingredients

1 (3 oz.) packages ramen noodles
1 C. cabbage, shredded
4 scallions, cut into 1 inch pieces
2-3 carrots
snow peas, julienned
3 tbsp mayonnaise
1/2 tsp sambal oelek, or sriracha

1-2 tsp lemon juice
1/4 C. peanuts, chopped
cilantro, chopped

Directions

1. Prepare the noodles according to the instructions on the package and cook it for 2 min. Remove it from the water and place it aside to drain.
2. Get a small mixing bowl: Whisk in it the mayo, sambal olek, and lemon juice to make the sauce
3. Get a large mixing bowl: Combine in it the cabbage, carrots, scallions, snow peas, cooked noodles, mayo sauce, a pinch of salt and pepper. Mix them well.
4. Serve your salad and enjoy.

CHILI RAMEN
Casserole

Prep Time: 5 mins
Total Time: 20 mins

Servings per Recipe: 4
Calories   502.3
Fat   24.1g
Cholesterol   54.2mg
Sodium   1979.9mg
Carbohydrates   55.0g
Protein   21.4g

Ingredients
3 packages ramen noodles
2 (15 oz.) cans chili with beans
1 (15 oz.) cans diced tomatoes
4 - 8 oz. shredded cheese

Directions
1. Pour 6 C. of water in a 3 quarts baking pan. Put on the lid and place it in the microwave for 3 to 4 min to heat up.
2. Use a rolling pan to crush the ramen slightly. Stir the noodles into the hot water of in the casserole.
3. Put on the lid and let it cook in the microwave for 2 min 30 sec. Stir the noodles and cook it for an extra 2 min 30 sec.
4. Discard the excess water from the casserole leaving the noodles in it. Add the tomatoes with chili and stir them well.
5. Cook them in the microwave on high for an extra 5 min. Top the ramen casserole with the shredded cheese.
6. Put on the lid and let it sit for several minutes until the cheese melts. Serve your casserole warm.
7. Enjoy.

Broccoli
and Oyster Ramen

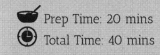 Prep Time: 20 mins

Total Time: 40 mins

Servings per Recipe: 4
Calories	575.7
Fat	32.8g
Cholesterol	75.9mg
Sodium	1207.9mg
Carbohydrates	41.4g
Protein	29.7g

Ingredients

1 lb boneless beef top sirloin steak
1 tbsp soy sauce
1 tbsp apple juice
2 tsp cornstarch
2 (3 oz.) packages beef-flavor ramen noodles
4 C. boiling water

2 tbsp olive oil
1 onion, chopped
3 C. frozen broccoli florets, thawed and drained
3 tbsp oyster sauce
1 tbsp cornstarch

Directions

1. Place the steak in the freezer until it is partially frozen then thinly slice it.
2. Get a large mixing bowl: Whisk in it the soy sauce, apple juice and 2 tsp cornstarch. Stir the beef into the mix.
3. Get a large mixing bowl: Crush the noodles into pieces stir it in it with the 1 seasoning packet.
4. Add 4 C. of water to the bowl and stir them. Cover the bowl and place it aside.
5. Place a large pan over high heat. Heat the oil in it. Sauté in it the beef for 3 min. Stir in the broccoli and cook it for 4 min.
6. Stir the beef into the skillet and cook them for 8 to 12 min.
7. Get a small mixing bowl: Whisk in it 1 C. of the ramen soaking liquid, oyster sauce, and 1 tbsp cornstarch.
8. Remove the noodles from the water and stir it into the skillet with oyster mix. Cook them until the ramen skillet thickens. Serve it warm.
9. Enjoy.

AUTHENTIC THAILAND
Rice Noodle Coconut Curry Soup

Prep Time: 15 mins
Total Time: 50 mins

Servings per Recipe: 4

Calories	247 kcal
Fat	13.1 g
Carbohydrates	23.8g
Protein	8.2 g
Cholesterol	30 mg
Sodium	1695 mg

Ingredients
2 oz. rice noodles
1 tbsp olive oil
1 clove garlic, minced
1 1/2 tbsp minced lemon grass
1 tsp ground ginger
2 tsp red curry paste, see appendix
1 (32 oz.) carton chicken broth
2 tbsp soy sauce
1 tbsp white sugar

1 (13.5 oz.) can reduced-fat coconut milk
1/2 C. peeled and deveined medium shrimp
1/2 C. sliced mushrooms
1 (10 oz.) bag baby spinach leaves
2 tbsp fresh lime juice
1/4 C. chopped cilantro
2 green onions, thinly sliced

Directions
1. In a large pan of lightly salted boiling water, cook the rice noodles for about 3 minutes.
2. Drain well and rinse under cold water to stop the cooking.
3. In a large pan, heat the oil on medium heat and sauté the garlic, lemon grass and ginger for about 30-60 seconds.
4. Add the curry paste and sauté for about 30 seconds.
5. Stir in about 1/2 C. of the chicken broth, remaining chicken stock, soy sauce and sugar and bring to a boil.
6. Reduce the heat to medium-low and simmer, partially covered for about 20 minutes.
7. Stir in the coconut milk, shrimp, mushrooms, spinach, lime juice and cilantro.
8. Increase the heat to medium-high and simmer for about 5 minutes.
9. Divide the rice noodles into serving bowl and top with the soup.
10. Serve with a garnishing of the sliced green onion.

Garden Zucchini and Onion Curry Soup

Prep Time: 15 mins
Total Time: 45 mins

Servings per Recipe: 6

Calories	74 kcal
Fat	5.2 g
Carbohydrates	6.3g
Protein	1.8 g
Cholesterol	< 1 mg
Sodium	< 537 mg

Ingredients

2 tbsp extra virgin olive oil
1 large onion, halved and thinly sliced
1 tbsp curry powder
Sea salt to taste

4 small zucchini, halved lengthwise and cut into 1 inch slices
1 quart chicken stock

Directions

1. In a large pan, heat the oil and sauté the onion, curry powder and salt till the onion becomes tender.
2. Stir in the zucchini and cook till tender.
3. Add the chicken stock and bring to a boil.
4. Reduce the heat to low and simmer, covered for about 20 minutes.
5. With a hand blender, blend the soup till smooth.

VERDANT CAYENNE
Cauliflower Curry Soup

🍳 Prep Time: 15 mins

🕐 Total Time: 1 hr 5 mins

Servings per Recipe: 4

Calories	359 kcal
Fat	32.7 g
Carbohydrates	15.1g
Protein	5.4 g
Cholesterol	90 mg
Sodium	1391 mg

Ingredients
1 head cauliflower, cut into florets
2 tbsp vegetable oil
1 tsp salt
1 tbsp butter, cut into small pieces
1 large yellow onion, diced
1 tsp chopped garlic
1 tsp curry powder

1 tsp cayenne pepper
1 tsp ground turmeric
1 quart chicken stock
1 C. heavy whipping cream
Salt and ground black pepper to taste
2 tbsp chopped fresh parsley

Directions
1. Set your oven to 450 degrees F before doing anything else.
2. In a bowl, add the cauliflower florets, vegetable oil and 1 tsp of the salt and toss o cot well.
3. Spread the cauliflower onto a baking sheet.
4. Cook in the oven for about 25 minutes.
5. In a large pan, melt the butter on medium heat and sauté the onion for about 5 minutes.
6. Stir in the garlic and sauté for about 2 minutes.
7. Stir in the curry powder, cayenne pepper and ground turmeric and sauté for about 5 minutes.
8. Stir in the roasted cauliflower and stock and bring to a boil.
9. Reduce the heat to low and simmer for about 10 minutes.
10. With an immersion blender, blend the mixture till smooth.
11. Stir in the cream, salt and pepper and remove from the heat.
12. Serve with a garnishing of the parsley.

Ginger Carrot Cashew and Onion Curry Soup

Prep Time: 20 mins
Total Time: 1 hr

Servings per Recipe: 6

Calories	317 kcal
Fat	26.7 g
Carbohydrates	19.8g
Protein	5.2 g
Cholesterol	0 mg
Sodium	473 mg

Ingredients

1 lb. carrots, peeled and cut in chunks
1 small onion, quartered
1/3 C. raw cashews
1 (14 oz.) can unsweetened light coconut milk

1 tsp curry powder
1/2 tsp ground ginger
1/2 tsp kosher salt
1 C. vegetable stock

Directions

1. Set your oven to 350 degrees F before doing anything else.
2. Arrange the carrots and onion in an ungreased shallow baking dish.
3. Cook in the oven for about 30‑35 minutes.
4. Remove from the oven and keep aside to cool slightly.
5. In a blender, add the cauliflower, cashews, coconut milk and seasonings and pulse till smooth.
6. Transfer the mixture into a medium pan with the stock on medium heat and cook for about 5 minutes.

CANADIAN GINGER
and Maple Sweet Potato Curry Soup

 Prep Time: 20 mins

Total Time: 7 hr 40 mins

Servings per Recipe: 9

Calories	159 kcal
Fat	3.5 g
Carbohydrates	28.9 g
Protein	3.3 g
Cholesterol	13 mg
Sodium	667 mg

Ingredients
5 C. chicken broth
2 large sweet potatoes, peeled and cut into cubes
2 C. baby carrots
1 onion, chopped
1 tsp red curry powder

3/4 tsp ground cinnamon
1/2 tsp ground ginger
1 C. half-and-half
2 tbsp real maple syrup
Salt and ground black pepper to taste

Directions
1. In a slow cooker, mix together the chicken broth, sweet potatoes, baby carrots, onion, red curry powder, cinnamon and ground ginger.
2. Set the slow cooker on Low and cook, covered for about 7 hours.
3. Remove from the heat and keep aside to cool slightly.
4. In a blender, add the mixture in batches and pulse till smooth.
5. Return the pureed soup into the slow cooker.
6. Stir in the half-and-half, maple syrup, salt and pepper.
7. Set the slow cooker on High and cook, covered for about 20 minutes.

Alternative
Cauliflower Curry Soup II

Prep Time: 15 mins
Total Time: 45 mins

Servings per Recipe: 8

Calories	75 kcal
Fat	3.8 g
Carbohydrates	9.6g
Protein	2.5 g
Cholesterol	4 mg
Sodium	403 mg

Ingredients

1 tbsp olive oil
1/2 onion, sliced
3 carrots cut into 1/2-inch slices
1/2 red bell pepper, sliced
3 cloves garlic, peeled
1 head cauliflower, chopped

1 (32 fluid oz.) container chicken stock
2 tbsp yellow curry powder
1 tbsp butter
4 dashes hot sauce
Salt and ground black pepper to taste

Directions

1. In a large pan, heat the oil on medium heat and sauté the onion, carrots, red bell pepper and garlic for about 5-10 minutes.
2. Add the cauliflower and chicken broth and bring to a boil.
3. Cook for about 10 minutes.
4. Remove from the heat and with a hand blender blend till smooth.
5. Return the pan on low heat and stir in the curry powder, butter, hot sauce, salt and pepper.
6. Simmer for about 15 minutes.
7. Serve hot.

VEGAN SPLIT PEAS
and Carrots
Curried

Prep Time: 20 mins
Total Time: 1 hr 25 mins

Servings per Recipe: 20
Calories	106 kcal
Fat	2.5 g
Carbohydrates	16.1g
Protein	5.6 g
Cholesterol	< 1 mg
Sodium	< 834 mg

Ingredients
3 tbsp olive oil
1/4 C. lemon juice
8 cloves garlic, minced
3 carrots, sliced
2 white onions, sliced
6 stalks celery, sliced
10 C. water
8 cubes chicken bouillon
2 C. dried split peas

1 tbsp Italian seasoning
1 tsp ground cumin
1 tbsp salt
1 tbsp ground black pepper
1/2 tsp cayenne pepper
4 tsp curry powder

Directions
1. In a large pan, heat the olive oil on medium heat and cook the lemon juice, garlic, carrots, onions and celery for about 20 minutes.
2. Transfer the vegetables and their juices into a bowl and refrigerate to cool slightly.
3. In a blender, add the mixture ad pulse till smooth.
4. In a large pan, dissolve the chicken bouillon cubes in the water on medium heat.
5. Add the vegetable puree and bring to a boil.
6. Stir in the split peas, Italian seasoning, cumin, salt, black pepper, cayenne pepper and curry powder.
7. Reduce the heat to medium-low and simmer for about 45 minutes.

Creamy
Lime Curry Soup

Prep Time: 15 mins
Total Time: 1 hr 20 mins

Servings per Recipe: 4	
Calories	229 kcal
Fat	10 g
Carbohydrates	35.3g
Protein	4.2 g
Cholesterol	13 mg
Sodium	353 mg

Ingredients

1 butternut squash, halved and seeded
1 tbsp olive oil
Salt and ground black pepper to taste
2 C. vegetable broth
1 tsp garlic powder
1 tsp onion powder

1 tsp curry powder
1/2 C. sour cream
1 tbsp lime juice
1 lime, zested

Directions

1. Set your oven to 350 degrees F before doing anything else and line a baking sheet with a piece of the foil.
2. Arrange the butternut squash onto the prepared baking sheet, cut-side up.
3. Coat the cut sides of squash with the olive oil and season with the salt and pepper.
4. Cook in the oven for about 45-60 minutes.
5. Remove the squash from the oven and keep aside to cool for about 10 minutes.
6. Scrape the flesh from the roasted butternut squash and transfer into a large pan with the broth, garlic powder, onion powder, curry powder, salt and pepper and bring to a simmer.
7. Simmer for about 10 minutes.
8. Remove from the heat and keep aside to cool slightly.
9. In a blender, add the soup mixture in batches and pulse till smooth.
10. In a bowl, add the sour cream, lime juice and lime zest and beat till well combined.
11. Serve the soup hot with a topping of the lime cream.

NORTHERN IRELAND
Inspired Leeks and Celery Curry Soup

Prep Time: 20 mins
Total Time: 1 hr

Servings per Recipe: 4

Calories	257 kcal
Fat	18.9 g
Carbohydrates	18.9 g
Protein	3.6 g
Cholesterol	16 mg
Sodium	798 mg

Ingredients
2 tbsp butter
3 leeks (white and pale green parts only), thinly sliced
1 clove garlic, minced
1 (32 fluid oz.) container chicken stock
1 1/2 C. thinly sliced carrots
2 stalks celery, thinly sliced
1 tsp curry powder

1/2 tsp ground turmeric
1/2 tsp ground ginger
1/8 tsp ground black pepper
1 pinch red pepper flakes
1 1/2 (12 oz.) cans light coconut milk

Directions
1. In a large pan, melt the butter on medium heat and sauté the leeks and garlic for about 5 minutes.
2. Stir in the chicken stock, carrots, celery, curry powder, turmeric, ginger, black pepper and red peppers flakes and bring to a boil.
3. Reduce the heat to medium-low and simmer, covered for about 30 minutes.
4. Stir in the coconut milk and simmer for about 1-2 minutes.

40-Minute
Curry Carrot Soup

Prep Time: 10 mins
Total Time: 40 mins

Servings per Recipe: 8

Calories	158 kcal
Fat	10.9 g
Carbohydrates	13.5g
Protein	3.1 g
Cholesterol	34 mg
Sodium	101 mg

Ingredients

2 tbsp olive oil
1 1/2 lb. peeled carrots, cut into 1-inch chunks
1 large onion, cut into large dice
1 tbsp butter
1 pinch sugar
3 large garlic cloves, thickly sliced

2 tbsp curry powder
3 C. chicken broth
1 1/2 C. half-and-half
Salt and freshly ground pepper, to taste
Garnish: chopped roasted pistachios

Directions

1. In a large sauté pan, heat the oil on medium-high heat and sauté the carrots and onion for about 7-8 minutes.
2. Reduce the heat to low and stir in the butter, sugar and garlic.
3. Cook for about 10 minutes, stirring occasionally.
4. Add the curry powder and sauté for about 30-60 seconds.
5. Increase the heat to medium-high.
6. Add the broth and bring to a boil.
7. Reduce the heat to low and simmer, partially covered for about 10 minutes.
8. With an immersion blender, blend till smooth.
9. Stir in the half-and-half, salt and pepper and cook till heated completely.
10. Serve with a garnishing of the roasted pistachios.

BANGKOK LIME
Tomato and Shrimp Curry Soup

Prep Time: 10 mins
Total Time: 45 mins

Servings per Recipe: 8

Calories	306 kcal
Fat	28.7 g
Carbohydrates	8.1g
Protein	19.2 g
Cholesterol	100 mg
Sodium	557 mg

Ingredients
1/4 C. red curry paste, see appendix
2 tbsp olive oil
3 C. coconut milk
3 C. chicken stock
2 limes, juiced
1 lime, zested
2 C. cherry tomatoes

1 tbsp chopped fresh cilantro
1 lb. shrimp
1 (14 oz.) can bean sprouts, drained
1 C. chopped cooked chicken
Salt and ground black pepper to taste

Directions
1. In a pan, mix together the red curry paste and olive oil on low heat and sauté for about 5 minutes.
2. Add the coconut milk, chicken stock, lime juice and lime zest and bring to a boil.
3. Reduce the heat to medium-low and simmer for about 10 minutes.
4. Stir in the cherry tomatoes and cilantro and again bring to a boil.
5. Simmer for about 10-15 minutes.
6. Stir in the shrimp, bean sprouts and cooked chicken and simmer for about 10-15 minutes.
7. Stir in the salt and pepper and serve.

Saturday Summer
Pumpkin Curry Soup

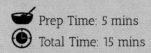 Prep Time: 5 mins

Total Time: 15 mins

Servings per Recipe: 4

Calories	81 kcal
Fat	2.9 g
Carbohydrates	12.7g
Protein	3 g
Cholesterol	10 mg
Sodium	1368 mg

Ingredients
1 (15 oz.) can pure pumpkin puree
2 C. Swanson(R) Chicken Broth
1/2 C. fat free half-and-half
1/2 tsp curry powder
1/8 tsp ground nutmeg

Salt and freshly ground black pepper to taste
1/4 C. reduced-fat sour cream
1 tbsp chopped fresh chives

Directions
1. In a medium pan, mix together the pumpkin puree and broth together on medium heat.
2. Stir in the half-and-half, curry powder, nutmeg, salt, and pepper and cook for about 10 minutes.
3. Serve with a garnishing of the sour cream and chopped chives.

PERSIAN INSPIRED
Saffron and Tomato Curry Soup

Prep Time: 15 mins
Total Time: 1 hr

Servings per Recipe: 4

Calories	222 kcal
Fat	19.9 g
Carbohydrates	8.8g
Protein	1.6 g
Cholesterol	15 mg
Sodium	217 mg

Ingredients

1 (14 oz.) can diced tomatoes, drained and juice reserved
1/4 C. extra virgin olive oil
Salt and black pepper to taste
2 tbsp butter
2 large pinches saffron
1 stalk celery, diced
1 small carrot, diced

1 yellow onion, diced
2 cloves garlic, minced
1 C. chicken broth
1/2 tsp curry powder
1 tsp lime juice
2 tbsp chopped cilantro

Directions

1. Set your oven to 350 degrees F before doing anything else.
2. Spread the drained tomatoes onto a rimmed baking sheet.
3. Drizzle with the olive oil and sprinkle with the salt and pepper.
4. Cook in the oven for about 20 minutes.
5. In a large pan, melt the butter on medium-low heat and sauté the saffron, celery, carrot, onion and garlic; for about 10 minutes.
6. Stir in the roasted tomatoes, reserved tomato juices and chicken broth and simmer for about 15-20 minutes.
7. Add the curry powder, lime juice and cilantro and stir to combine.
8. With an immersion blender, blend the soup till smooth.
9. Serve immediately.

Okanagan Fruity
Madras Peach Soup Curry

🥣 Prep Time: 25 mins

🕐 Total Time: 1 hr 10 mins

Servings per Recipe: 4	
Calories	523 kcal
Fat	40.4 g
Carbohydrates	26.3g
Protein	17.5 g
Cholesterol	206 mg
Sodium	437 mg

Ingredients

5 tbsp olive oil
2 tbsp Madras curry powder
1 large onion, minced
3 cloves garlic, minced
1 (15 oz.) can sliced peaches in syrup, chopped
1 (14.5 oz.) can chopped plum tomatoes
1 tsp ground ginger

1 C. cream
1 C. vegetable broth
Salt and black pepper to taste
2 C. lettuce, chopped
2 C. shelled, cooked shrimp

Directions

1. In a large pan, heat the oil on medium heat and sauté the curry powder for about 1 minute.
2. Add the onion and garlic and cook for about 8-10 minutes.
3. Stir in the peaches with syrup, tomatoes, ginger, cream, broth, salt and pepper.
4. Reduce the heat to low and simmer for about 45 minutes.
5. Serve hot with a topping of the shrimp and lettuce.

PASTORAL MUSHROOM and Rice Curry Soup

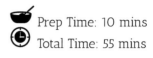 Prep Time: 10 mins
Total Time: 55 mins

Servings per Recipe: 7	
Calories	176 kcal
Fat	9 g
Carbohydrates	19.2g
Protein	4.1 g
Cholesterol	25 mg
Sodium	456 mg

Ingredients
1 C. uncooked wild rice
1/4 C. butter
1 onion, chopped
2 1/2 C. sliced fresh mushrooms
1/2 C. chopped celery
1/2 C. all-purpose flour
6 C. vegetable broth
2 C. half-and-half
2/3 C. dry sherry

1/2 tsp salt
1/2 tsp white pepper
1/2 tsp curry powder
1/2 tsp dry mustard
1/2 tsp paprika
1/2 tsp dried chervil
1 tbsp chopped fresh parsley, for garnish

Directions
1. In a pan of the boiling water, stir in the rice.
2. Reduce the heat and simmer, covered for about 40 minutes.
3. In a large pan, melt the butter on medium heat and sauté the onion till golden brown.
4. Add the mushrooms and celery and sauté for about 2 minutes.
5. Reduce the heat to low.
6. Stir in the flour and cook till the mixture becomes bubbly, stirring continuously.
7. Slowly, add the broth, stirring continuously.
8. Increase the heat to medium-high and bring to a boil, stirring continuously.
9. Reduce the heat to low and stir in the cooked rice, half and half, sherry, salt, white pepper, curry powder, dry mustard, paprika and chervil.
10. Simmer till heated completely.
11. Serve hot with a garnishing of the parsley.

Agrarian
Mustard Seed Curry Soup

🥣 Prep Time: 10 mins
🕐 Total Time: 1 hr

Servings per Recipe: 8	
Calories	157 kcal
Fat	12 g
Carbohydrates	9.5g
Protein	3.9 g
Cholesterol	25 mg
Sodium	825 mg

Ingredients

1 head cauliflower, cut into florets
2 tbsp olive oil
2 tsp curry powder
2 tsp mustard seeds
5 tbsp butter, divided
1/3 C. chopped sweet onion

6 C. chicken broth
3 tbsp all-purpose flour
1 C. milk
Salt and ground black pepper to taste

Directions

1. Set your oven to 350 degrees F before doing anything else.
2. In a baking dish, add the cauliflower, olive oil, curry powder and mustard seeds and toss to coat.
3. Cook in the oven for about 35-40 minutes.
4. In a large pan, melt 2 tbsp of the butter on medium heat and sauté the onion for about 5-10 minutes.
5. Add the chicken broth and cauliflower and bring to a boil.
6. Reduce heat to low and simmer.
7. Meanwhile for the roux in a small pan, mix together 3 tbsp of the butter and flour on medium-low heat.
8. Cook for about 5 minutes, stirring continuously.
9. Stir in the milk to roux and cook for about 5-10 minutes, stirring continuously.
10. Add the roux into the soup and stir till smooth.
11. Stir in the salt and pepper and serve.

LIGHT COCONUT
Curry Soup for Mid-October

Prep Time: 20 mins
Total Time: 50 mins

Servings per Recipe: 6
Calories   171 kcal
Fat   13.5 g
Carbohydrates   12g
Protein   2 g
Cholesterol   0 mg
Sodium   601 mg

Ingredients
1/4 C. coconut oil
1 C. chopped onions
1 clove garlic, minced
3 C. vegetable broth
1 tsp curry powder
1/2 tsp salt

1/4 tsp ground coriander
1/4 tsp crushed red pepper flakes
1 (15 oz.) can pure pumpkin
1 C. light coconut milk

Directions
1. In a large pan, melt the coconut oil on medium heat and sauté the onions and garlic for about 5 minutes.
2. Stir in the vegetable broth, curry powder, salt, coriander and red pepper flakes and bring to a gentle boil.
3. Cook for about 10 minutes.
4. Cook, covered for about 15-20 minutes, stirring occasionally.
5. Stir in the pumpkin and coconut milk and cook for about 5 minutes.
6. Remove from the heat and keep aside to cool slightly.
7. In a blender, add the soup in batches and pulse till smooth.
8. Return the pureed soup into the pan on medium heat and cook till heated completely.

Squash, Rice, Lentils and Macaroni Curry Soup Dinner

🥣 Prep Time: 20 mins
🕐 Total Time: 1 hr 30 mins

Servings per Recipe: 7

Calories	166 kcal
Fat	3.6 g
Carbohydrates	28.6g
Protein	5.5 g
Cholesterol	0 mg
Sodium	572 mg

Ingredients

- 1 onion, chopped
- 3 cloves crushed garlic
- 1 tbsp olive oil
- 1 1/2 tsp curry powder
- 1 tsp ground cumin
- 1 tsp ground turmeric
- 8 C. vegetable stock
- 1/4 C. dry lentils
- 1 (28 oz.) can diced tomatoes with juice
- 1/4 C. uncooked white rice
- 1 C. frozen corn
- 1/4 C. elbow macaroni
- 1 small spaghetti squash

Directions

1. Set your oven to 350 degrees F before doing anything else and lightly, grease a baking dish.
2. Arrange the squash in the prepared baking dish, cut side down.
3. Cook in the oven for about 30 minutes.
4. Remove from the oven and keep aside to cool slightly.
5. With a fork, shred the squash.
6. In a large pan, heat the oil and sauté the onion and garlic till tender.
7. Stir in the curry powder, cumin and turmeric and sauté till translucent.
8. Add the stock and lentils and bring to a boil.
9. Reduce the heat to low and stir in the chopped tomatoes with juice.
10. Simmer for about 25 minutes.
11. Stir in the rice and corn and simmer for about 35 minutes.
12. Stir in the macaroni and shredded squash and simmer till cook till desired doneness of the rice and macaroni.

HOW TO MAKE
a Simple Curry Soup

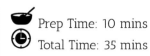 Prep Time: 10 mins

Total Time: 35 mins

Servings per Recipe: 8
Calories	161 kcal
Fat	11.1 g
Carbohydrates	15.4g
Protein	2.7 g
Cholesterol	0 mg
Sodium	317 mg

Ingredients
4 C. vegetable broth
2 tsp curry powder
1 tsp ground cumin
1/2 tsp ground cinnamon
1/2 tsp ground ginger
2 lb. carrots, peeled and chopped

1 (14 oz.) can coconut milk
14 oz. water
1 tsp chopped fresh cilantro

Directions
1. In a large pan, add the vegetable broth on medium heat and bring to a boil.
2. Stir in the curry powder, cumin, cinnamon, ginger and carrots.
3. Reduce the heat and simmer for about 20 minutes, stirring occasionally.
4. Drain the carrots, reserving about 1/4 C. of the vegetable broth.
5. Keep aside to cool slightly.
6. In a blender, add the carrots and reserved broth in batches and pulses till smooth.
7. Return the carrots into the pan with the coconut milk and water and bring to a simmer.
8. Serve with a garnishing of the cilantro.

Tuesday's
Curried Beef Soup

Prep Time: 15 mins
Total Time: 1 hr 30 mins

Servings per Recipe: 6

Calories	343 kcal
Fat	19.8 g
Carbohydrates	20.5g
Protein	20 g
Cholesterol	61 mg
Sodium	939 mg

Ingredients

2 tbsp butter
2 onions, chopped
1 lb. cubed beef stew meat
6 C. beef stock
2 tbsp curry powder

2 bay leaves
2 potatoes, sliced
2 tbsp distilled white vinegar
2 tsp salt

Directions

1. In a large pan, melt the butter and cook the onions and beef cubes till the beef is browned completely.
2. Add the beef stock, curry powder and bay leaves and stir to combine.
3. Reduce the heat to low and simmer for about for 30 minutes.
4. Add the potatoes, vinegar and salt and simmer for about 45-60 minutes.
5. Discard the bay leaves and serve hot.

BROCCOLI, CELERY
Lentils, and
Potato Curry Soup

🥣 Prep Time: 25 mins
🕐 Total Time: 1 hr 15 mins

Servings per Recipe: 10
Calories   200 kcal
Fat   3.5 g
Carbohydrates   32.8g
Protein   9.6 g
Cholesterol   0 mg
Sodium   250 mg

Ingredients
2 tbsp olive oil
1 onion, diced
3 cloves garlic, chopped
1 C. broccoli florets
4 stalks celery, chopped
1 baking potato, peeled

5 C. vegetable broth
1 1/2 C. cooked white rice
1 1/2 C. uncooked green lentils
2 tsp curry powder

Directions
1. In a large pan, heat the oil on medium heat and sauté the onion, garlic, broccoli and celery till tender.
2. Remove from the heat and keep aside to cool slightly.
3. In a microwave safe bowl, place the potato and microwave for about 5-10 minutes.
4. In a food processor, add the potato and broccoli mixture and pulse till smooth.
5. Transfer the mixture into the pan and bring to a boil.
6. Add the cooked rice, lentils and curry powder and stir to combine.
7. Reduce the heat to low and simmer, covered for about 45 minutes.

Simply Spinach and Potato Curry Soup

Prep Time: 15 mins
Total Time: 35 mins

Servings per Recipe: 8
Calories	181 kcal
Fat	10.5 g
Carbohydrates	18.1g
Protein	4.7 g
Cholesterol	4 mg
Sodium	84 mg

Ingredients

1 large potato - peeled and cubed
6 tbsp olive oil
1/2 C. chopped green onions
12 C. spinach - rinsed, stemmed, and dried
1/3 C. all-purpose flour

2 tsp curry powder
4 C. chicken broth
1 tbsp lemon juice
1 (8 oz.) carton nonfat sour cream

Directions

1. In a pan, add the potato and enough water to cover and bring to a boil.
2. Cook till the potato becomes tender.
3. Drain the potato and keep aside.
4. In a large pan, heat 2 tbsp of the oil and sauté the green onions till tender.
5. Stir in the cooked potato.
6. Slowly, stir in the spinach, stirring after each addition till the spinach is wilted.
7. Remove from the heat and keep aside to cool slightly.
8. In a blender, add the soup in batches and pulse till smooth.
9. In the same pan, heat the remaining olive oil.
10. Stir in the flour and curry powder till well combined
11. Slowly, add the broth, stirring continuously.
12. Stir in the spinach mixture and lemon juice and bring to a boil on medium heat, stirring continuously.
13. In a bowl, place the sour cream.
14. Add about 1 C. of the hot soup and mix till well combined.

15. Add the sour cream mixture into the simmering soup and stir to combine.
16. Cook till heated completely.
17. Serve immediately.

Apple and Leeks
with Potatoes Curried Soup

Prep Time: 10 mins
Total Time: 36 mins

Servings per Recipe: 4

Calories	133 kcal
Fat	3.6 g
Carbohydrates	23.9g
Protein	2.9 g
Cholesterol	< 1 mg
Sodium	< 395 mg

Ingredients

1 tbsp margarine
2 tsp curry powder
3 leeks, chopped
3/4 C. diced potatoes
2 Granny Smith apples -- peeled, cored
and chopped
3 C. vegetable broth
Salt and pepper to taste
1/4 C. plain yogurt

Directions

1. In a medium pan, melt the butter on medium heat and sauté the curry powder for about 1 minute.
2. Stir in the leeks, potato and apples and cook for about 5 minutes.
3. Stir in the broth and bring to a boil.
4. Reduce the heat and simmer, covered for about 20 minutes.
5. Remove from the heat and keep aside to cool slightly.
6. In a blender, add the soup in batches and pulse till smooth.
7. Stir in the salt and pepper.
8. Serve immediately with a swirl of the yogurt.

PUMPKIN AND APPLE
for Early November Curry Soup

Prep Time: 20 mins

Total Time: 1 hr 10 mins

Servings per Recipe: 6	
Calories	131 kcal
Fat	3.4 g
Carbohydrates	22.6g
Protein	4.7 g
Cholesterol	5 mg
Sodium	696 mg

Ingredients

4 Macintosh apples - peeled, cored and chopped
1 tbsp butter
1 onion, finely chopped
2 cloves garlic, crushed
1 tbsp curry powder
1 tsp ground cumin

1 (15 oz.) can pumpkin puree
4 C. chicken broth
1 C. water
1 tsp white sugar

Directions

1. In a large pan, melt the butter on medium heat and sauté the onion, garlic, curry powder and cumin till the onion becomes soft.
2. Stir in the apples, pumpkin, broth, water and sugar and bring to a boil, stirring occasionally.
3. Reduce the heat to low and simmer, covered for about 25 minutes, stirring occasionally.
4. Remove from the heat and keep aside to cool slightly.
5. In a blender, add the soup in batches and pulse till smooth.
6. Return the soup to pan on low heat and cook, covered till heated completely.
7. Serve hot.

Beautiful Pear and Ginger Curry Soup

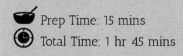 Prep Time: 15 mins

Total Time: 1 hr 45 mins

Servings per Recipe: 8	
Calories	167 kcal
Fat	6.6 g
Carbohydrates	27.5g
Protein	3 g
Cholesterol	20 mg
Sodium	786 mg

Ingredients

1 (2 lb.) butternut squash
3 tbsp unsalted butter
1 onion, diced
2 cloves garlic, minced
2 tsp minced fresh ginger root
1 tbsp curry powder

1 tsp salt
4 C. reduced sodium chicken broth
2 firm ripe Bartlett pears, peeled, cored, and cut into 1 inch dice
1/2 C. half and half

Directions

1. Set your oven to 450 degrees F before doing anything else and line a rimmed baking sheet with a parchment paper.
2. Cut the squash in half lengthwise.
3. Remove the seeds and membrane.
4. Arrange the squash halves onto the prepared baking sheet, cut sides down.
5. Cook in the oven for about 45 minutes.
6. Remove from the oven and scoop the flesh from the squash halves.
7. In a large pan, melt the butter on medium heat and sauté the onion, garlic, ginger, curry powder and salt for about 10 minutes.
8. Add the chicken broth and bring to a boil.
9. Stir in the pears and squash flesh and simmer for about 30 minutes.
10. Remove from the heat and keep aside to cool slightly.
11. In a blender, add the soup in batches and pulse till smooth.
12. Return the soup to the pan and stir in the half and half.
13. Cook till heated completely.
14. Serve hot.

TROPICAL COCONUT and Lime Curry Soup

🍲 Prep Time: 10 mins
🕐 Total Time: 1 hr 10 mins

Servings per Recipe: 6
Calories	143 kcal
Fat	9.8 g
Carbohydrates	13.4g
Protein	3 g
Cholesterol	0 mg
Sodium	680 mg

Ingredients
6 carrots, peeled and chopped
1/2 head cauliflower, trimmed and chopped
1 1/2 tsp olive oil
2 cloves garlic, chopped
1 tsp salt
1 tsp ground black pepper

3 C. vegetable broth
1 tbsp curry powder
1 C. coconut milk
1/2 lime, juiced

Directions
1. Set your oven to 400 degrees F before doing anything else.
2. In a casserole dish, add the carrots, cauliflower, olive oil, garlic, salt and black pepper and toss to coat well.
3. Cook in the oven for about 45 minutes, stirring once after 20 minutes.
4. Remove from the oven and stir well.
5. In a large pan, add the vegetable broth and bring to a boil.
6. Stir in the curry powder and roasted vegetables and bring to a boil.
7. Cook, covered for about 8-10 minutes.
8. Remove from the heat.
9. With an immersion blender, blend the soup till smooth.
10. Return the pan on medium heat.
11. Stir in the coconut milk and lime juice and simmer for about 5-10 minutes.
12. Serve hot.

I Love
Curry Soup

Prep Time: 15 mins
Total Time: 2 hr 30 mins

Servings per Recipe: 6

Calories	315 kcal
Fat	22.8 g
Carbohydrates	27.6g
Protein	6.5 g
Cholesterol	10 mg
Sodium	624 mg

Ingredients

1 butternut squash, halved and seeded
1 tbsp butter, melted
1 tsp salt, divided
3/4 tsp pumpkin pie spice, divided
1/4 tsp cayenne pepper
1 tbsp butter
1/2 C. chopped yellow onion

1 tsp yellow curry powder
1 (13 oz.) can coconut milk
2 1/2 C. vegetable stock
1/4 tsp freshly grated nutmeg
1/2 C. pepitas (pumpkin seeds)
1 pinch freshly grated nutmeg

Directions

1. Set your oven to 425 degrees F before doing anything else.
2. Arrange the butternut squash in a baking dish, flesh side up.
3. Coat the flesh of squash with 1 tbsp of the melted butter and sprinkle with 1/2 tsp of the salt, 1/2 tsp of the pumpkin pie spice and cayenne pepper.
4. Cook in the oven for about 1 hour.
5. Remove the squash from the oven and keep aside to cool for about 15 minutes.
6. Scoop flesh from the butternut squash.
7. In a large pan, melt 1 tbsp of the butter on medium heat and sauté the onion for about 2 minutes.
8. Add the curry powder and sauté for about 1 minute.
9. Stir in the coconut milk and bring to a boil.
10. Add the squash flesh, remaining 1/2 tsp of the salt, 1/4 tsp pumpkin pie spice, vegetable stock, and 1/4 tsp of the nutmeg and bring to a boil.
11. Reduce the heat to low and simmer till heated completely.
12. With an immersion blender, blend the soup on low speed till smooth.

13. Simmer for about 20 minutes.
14. Stir in the salt and remove from the heat.
15. Serve hot with a topping of the pepitas and a pinch of nutmeg.

Full
Hanoi Curried Soup

🍜 Prep Time: 30 mins
🕐 Total Time: 2 hr 30 mins

Servings per Recipe: 8

Calories	512 kcal
Fat	26.8 g
Carbohydrates	40.6g
Protein	29.8 g
Cholesterol	75 mg
Sodium	374 mg

Ingredients

2 tbsp vegetable oil
1 (3 lb.) whole chicken, skin removed and cut into pieces
1 onion, cut into chunks
2 shallots, thinly sliced
2 cloves garlic, chopped
1/8 C. thinly sliced fresh ginger root
1 stalk lemon grass, cut into 2 inch pieces
4 tbsp curry powder
1 green bell pepper, cut into 1 inch pieces
2 carrots, sliced diagonally

1 quart chicken broth
1 quart water
2 tbsp fish sauce
2 kaffir lime leaves
1 bay leaf
2 tsp red pepper flakes
8 small potatoes, quartered
1 (14 oz.) can coconut milk
1 bunch fresh cilantro

Directions

1. In a large pan, heat the oil on medium heat and cook the chicken and onion till the onion becomes translucent.
2. Transfer the chicken mixture into a bowl and keep aside.
3. In the same pan, add the shallots and sauté for about 1 minute.
4. Stir in the garlic, ginger, lemon grass and curry powder and cook for about 5 minutes.
5. Stir in the bell peppers, carrots, chicken mixture, chicken broth, water, fish sauce, lime leaves, bay leaf and red pepper flakes and bring to a boil.
6. Stir in the potatoes and again bring to a boil.
7. Stir in the coconut milk.
8. Reduce the heat and simmer for about 40-60 minutes.
9. Serve with a garnishing of the fresh cilantro sprigs.

LINDA-MAE'S
Secret Curry Soup

🍲 Prep Time: 15 mins
🕐 Total Time: 1 hr 45 mins

Servings per Recipe: 4
Calories	388 kcal
Fat	25.1 g
Carbohydrates	44.3g
Protein	5.7 g
Cholesterol	0 mg
Sodium	68 mg

Ingredients
1 butternut squash
1 tbsp olive oil
1 onion, chopped
1 shallot, minced
2 tbsp curry powder
1 tsp ground turmeric

1 apple, cored and chopped
1 slice fresh ginger, minced
Water to cover
1 (14 oz.) can coconut milk
Salt to taste

Directions
1. Set your oven to 350 degrees F before doing anything else.
2. With a fork, pierce the butternut squash and arrange onto a baking sheet.
3. Cook in the oven for about 45 minutes.
4. Remove from the oven and keep aside to cool slightly.
5. Cut the squash in half.
6. Peel, scoop the seeds and chop the flesh.
7. In a skillet, heat the olive oil on medium heat and sauté the onion and shallot for about 10 minutes.
8. Add the curry powder and turmeric and sauté for about 2 minutes.
9. Stir in the squash, apple, ginger and enough water to cover and bring to a boil.
10. Reduce the heat to medium-low and simmer for about 15 minutes.
11. With an immersion blender, blend till the squash is broken into pieces.
12. Stir in the coconut milk and salt and simmer for about 3 minutes.

Restaurant Style
Shallot and Ginger Curry Soup

Prep Time: 15 mins
Total Time: 50 mins

Servings per Recipe: 5
Calories	131 kcal
Fat	2.1 g
Carbohydrates	23.1g
Protein	5.7 g
Cholesterol	0 mg
Sodium	539 mg

Ingredients
2 tsp canola oil
1/2 C. chopped shallots
3 C. 1/2-inch cubes peeled sweet potato
1 1/2 C. 1/4-inch slices peeled carrot
1 tbsp grated fresh ginger root

2 tsp curry powder
3 C. fat free, low-sodium chicken broth
1/2 tsp salt

Directions
1. In a large pan, heat the oil on medium-high heat and sauté the shallots for about 3 minutes.
2. Stir in the sweet potato, carrot, ginger and curry powder and sauté for about 3-4 minutes.
3. Add the chicken broth and bring to a boil.
4. Reduce the heat to low and simmer, covered for about 25-30 minutes.
5. Stir in the salt.
6. Remove from the heat and keep aside to cool slightly.
7. In a blender, add the soup in batches and pulse till smooth.
8. Serve immediately.

Manufactured by Amazon.ca
Bolton, ON